ICE POP JOY

ICE POP JOY

ORGANIC · HEALTHY · FRESH · DELICIOUS

ANNI DAULTER
photographs by Alexandra DeFurio

SELLERS
PUBLISHING

Dedication

This book is dedicated to my family: my loving husband, Tim, and my children, Zoë, Lotus, Bodhi, and River. I love you all so much and want to thank you for tasting all my pops, taking pictures, and being patient with me through this process.

Anni (aka: mom)

For my beloved daughters, Bella and Sophia.

Alexandra DeFurio

Published by Sellers Publishing, Inc.

Text and photographs copyright © 2011 Anni Daulter
All food styling by Anni Daulter
All rights reserved.

Sellers Publishing, Inc.
161 John Roberts Road, South Portland, Maine 04106
Visit our Web site: www.sellerspublishing.com • E-mail: rsp@rsvp.com

ISBN: 13: 978-1-4162-0625-5
Library of Congress Control Number: 2010933891

10 9 8 7 6 5 4 3 2 1

Printed and bound in China.

CONTENTS

Preface

My love for cooking came from my desire to make healthy foods that my kids would actually want to eat. When I wrote my first book, *Organically Raised: Conscious Cooking for Babies and Toddlers*, I included a sweets and snacks section that was filled with treats for kids that parents would actually feel good about giving their families. My inspiration for *Ice Pop Joy* came from that same desire to find more wholesome snacks and desserts for my children to enjoy.

I wrote this book for parents who stay awake at night worried that their children aren't getting enough protein or veggies because their kids flat out refuse to eat them. As a mom, I've had those concerns and know how frustrating it can be to try to get kids to eat something when they're not in the mood.

We need as many tools in our parenting bag as we can get. *Ice Pop Joy* is the secret weapon you've been waiting for. These recipes will encourage your kids to try new flavors and appreciate fresh, seasonal ingredients. Before you know it, your kids will be creating their own signature frozen treats filled with their own choice wholesome ingredients and sharing them with their friends!

Anni

Welcome to Ice Pop Joy

This book is packed with recipes that will give you many healthy frozen treat ideas that your entire family will love. As a concerned mom, I understand how much time we parents spend worrying about what our kids are eating and if they are getting enough vitamins and protein in their meals. Plus, there is the frequent battle with what to serve for a "treat." These ice pops showcase great alternatives to refined sugar desserts and snacks lacking any nutritional value. In general, I say stick to the "Positive 4" rule. Try to keep your treats organic, healthy, fresh, and delicious.

Organic

Eating organic means no pesticides or toxic chemicals in the food. This is especially important for children because we don't know what the long-term health effects of pesticides truly are. Because non-organic fruits and vegetables tend to have higher toxicity levels than other foods, it's especially important to buy those items organic as much as possible. According to the Environmental Protection Agency (EPA), as much as 1.5 billion pounds of pesticides are used on crops yearly. When you shop at your local farmers' market, it's easy to find seasonal organic produce at affordable prices. Although it is important to buy organic fruits and vegetables, it is equally important to buy as many other organic ingredients as possible. Look for organic nuts and dairy products, too, when choosing ingredients for your ice pops.

Healthy

Many parents struggle with getting their children to eat nutritious foods. It is easy to get frustrated and eventually give up. *Ice Pop Joy* is the perfect fix. None of the recipes include refined sugar; instead many use agave nectar, honey, or no added sweetener at all. What's more, many boosters such as herbs, nuts, seeds, wheat germ, and tofu are used to increase the overall health benefits of the pops.

Fresh

Buying fresh, local, seasonal ingredients makes all the difference when creating great foods. Fresh foods just taste better! In order to get the freshest fare possible, try buying produce at your local farmers' market, or better yet, have your children help you plant a small garden of your own. This may sound like a huge undertaking, but you don't need a huge space to do it. You can easily and simply grow herbs and vegetables in window boxes or pots. Growing even a little of your own food shows your children where their food comes from and how delicious really fresh produce can be! I've found that if kids feel connected to the food, they're more likely to be interested in eating it (this is true of even the fussiest of eaters!). If your region's climate doesn't allow for local fresh fruits and vegetables in the colder months, consider freezing a variety of produce when it is in season. There are also plenty of pop recipes within the following chapters that use mainly yogurt, tofu, and herbal teas, which can be fresh in any season.

Delicious

I am a firm believer in "yumminess" and if the ice pop doesn't taste great, kids won't eat it. (My taste-testing children have taught me that!) Many people automatically equate healthy recipes with food that's not fun to eat, but that's not the case with these tasty treats. The right combinations really make the difference. You'll be surprised to find your kids falling in love with complex flavors and eventually coming up with their own unique combinations. Before you know it, they'll expand their culinary palates by demanding more!

Help, I Can't Get My Kids to Eat Anything Healthy!

I cannot tell you how many times I've heard parents say that they just cannot get their kids to eat healthy foods. They struggle with ideas and worry that their children aren't getting enough vegetables or protein. The truth is, even if they are picky eaters now, your kids will eventually expand their tastes. As children grow and change, so will their likes and dislikes. In the meantime, get creative and be patient. Even if your child doesn't start off eating a variety of produce and flavors, it's never too late to start over. Here are some ideas to help you help them!

Quick Tips about "starting over" with healthy foods with your children

- Don't hide the ingredients from them. Let them see what you're making the pops out of and talk about ingredients with your children.

- Ask for their suggestions on creating a signature "veggie" pop that you can name after them, and even submit to me for a fun addition to my Web site, under the section "kids' corner."

- Offering your children more exotic or unusual ingredients through ice pops may be just what is needed to help them be a tad more adventurous. Flavors are often less intense when they are icy cold, so ice pops with healthy ingredients can be a great starting point for new flavors.

- Have your children be active participants in choosing ingredients for your pops at the farmers' market, perhaps even carrying their own baskets for their selections.

- After your children have enjoyed their veggie pops, let them help you prepare the same vegetables with you for dinner so they can see and try the same veggies again in a variety of ways.

- Keep offering! Allow your children the room to express likes and dislikes, but keep trying with veggies, as childrens' tastes change as often as they do.

- Sometimes an unusual texture leads to the "ewww" response from children. You can easily change the texture of some high-nutrient foods — such as tofu or kale — by blending them into your pops.

- Introduce "fairy bites." We always ask our children to try at least a little "fairy bite" of whatever we have made so they can go back and report to the fairy world whether there is a good new recipe hitting the "human world." It works for us; it might also work for you.

- If your kids do not like traditional protein sources, using nuts and various grains in your pops will help get those proteins in and will add flavor and crunch to your favorite pops.

Pop Practicalities

Molds

Stainless steel:

Check these out! The only stainless steel ice pop molds I have found on the market are ONYX brand, and I love them. They are eco-friendly, easy to use, freeze super-fast, and were made by a mom who wanted better products for her kids. ONYX also makes stainless steel ice cube trays, which you can also use for ice pop molds as well.

BPA-free plastic molds:

Bisphenol A, also known as BPA, is a toxic chemical that manufacturers often use in polycarbonate plastics found in baby bottles and sippy cups. Early over-exposure to the chemical can have lifelong health effects.(1) There are many BPA-free pop molds out there. You can find several choices in various shapes and sizes online or local shops.

Creative options:

You can also go to your local kitchen store and try to find molds used for other things like baking. You can use paper cups, which come in various sizes, or even try a baking loaf pan that you cut into square pieces. (NOTE: For the baking pan, you will have to let your pop liquid slightly freeze before placing your sticks where you want them, so they will have a firm base to stand straight.) You may be able to get really creative and find many more interesting shapes to have fun with.

Other Equipment Needed

Blender:

A blender is critical in making nice smooth pops! You will use a blender for almost all your ice pop creations, so it's a good investment.

Food processor:

You can also use a food processor to blend your ingredients for your pops. It will allow you more flexibility in preserving some texture, because you may want some of your pops to have a little crunch. It's easier to get textured blends with a food processor than it is with a blender. But if you only have a food processor, it can be substituted for a blender, because you can obtain a completely smooth texture if desired.

Steamer:

A vegetable steamer is important because some recipes require vegetables and fruits to be lightly steamed before creating your pop. A lightly steamed vegetable or fruit will be a little softer and therefore easier to blend with the other ingredients.

Wooden sticks:

I like using wooden popsicle sticks to make my pops because I feel they lend an authentic and natural look to the finished pop. You can buy the sticks at your local art or craft store or online, and you can get lots inexpensively. Some ice pop molds come with sticks and lids.

Popsicle maker:

Now I have seen everything! There is a ice pop maker on the market and it works to freeze your pops in 7 minutes. This contraption is a lot of fun for the kids and is a particularly good idea for pop parties. Williams Sonoma makes this fast-pace pop maker. I tried it, and I have to admit I found it a bit addicting.

Freezing

Give your pops plenty of time to freeze. If you are making layered pops, you have to freeze the pop layer by layer until each layer is hard enough to handle the next layer being poured on it without mixing in. If the first layer is too soft, your ice pop won't have distinctive layers. It is also important to remember that you have to wait until the pop liquid has frozen enough to support your pop stick so that it can stand up straight. The amount of time it takes a pop to partially freeze (enough to hold up a stick) or completely freeze depends on the ingredients in the pop and the temperature of your freezer. I often turn up my freezer to make it even a little colder if I want to make pops faster. If you are using pop molds complete with sticks and lids, you will be able to insert the stick immediately (before the pop is even partially frozen) since the lid holds the stick in place.

Pop Sweeteners

Nature's Nectar: Honey, Agave, & Coconut Sugar

Sweeteners can be a tricky subject for health-conscious folks. Sweeteners are meant to sweeten our foods and make certain foods more palatable. No sweetener is particularly healthy and none qualifies as a superfood; therefore, all sweeteners should be employed in moderation. Many of the ice pops in this book do not use any additional sweeteners and are sweetened with the natural sugars from the fruits themselves. Some ingredients don't have a natural sweetness and need a little extra boost to make them delectable. As a concerned mother, I want to make sure I am educated about what I feed my family. I want to avoid the highly processed refined sugars that are the mainstream sweeteners on the market. When it comes to sweeteners, some products are better than others. Here are some alternative sweeteners that you'll find in the recipes throughout this collection:

Honey truly is nature's nectar, and thanks to the bees, we have this delicious sticky, gooey sweetener that not only tastes great, but has some health benefits as well. When I visited my friend Lynn, who is a beekeeper, to get some photos of her beautiful golden honey and to ask her about the ins and outs of honey making, I learned a lot and I even got stung, which she said was good for me. Honey is a natural sweetener, and if you can get it straight from a local farmer, you will get the raw honey that has not been processed or treated and can help with ailments like allergies. Honey has a low glycemic index, which means it does not produce the sugar highs that processed sugars do. Honey is also a natural antioxidant so it can boost your immune system. Honey is great as an alternative to sugar, but also can be great for healing open wounds, and it is a miracle for sore throats. Honey, however, is not suitable for babies under age one, as they do not have a fully developed digestive system and could be subjected to infant botulism food poisoning.

Raw agave nectar or syrup, which comes from a plant that resembles an aloe, is another great sweetener alternative with a low glycemic index and high antioxidant properties. Raw agave that has been minimally processed at low temperatures with non GM (genetically modified) vegan enzymes and that has been collected by indigenous people from live plants, is the best. This type of processing keeps the fructose levels closer to what is naturally found in the plant and maintains its nutrients and enzymes. The great thing about agave is that this liquid gold is so sweet on its own, you can use about half of what you would use with refined table sugars. It's thinner than honey and now is widely available in most grocery stores and easy to buy online as well. The best raw agave comes from the salmiana agave plant; my favorite companies that sell this type are Madhava and Loving Earth (see the Resource section in the back of this book).

Coconut sugar comes from coconut palm sugar blossoms. This sugar has a low glycemic index. It's organic, unprocessed, unfiltered, and unbleached. It's available online and at most natural or health food stores.

It just goes to show us that nature has a simple solution for meeting our sweet-tooth needs, and highly refined sugars do not need to be present in our diet if we utilize these alternatives.

Pure Fruit Pops

This chapter features a collection of classic fruit pops,
each with a surprising twist that takes the flavor
from refreshing to amazing!

Fruit Basics:

Most children like fruit and will readily consume it due to its natural sweetness. Always buy fruits when they are in season, and buy fruits grown locally whenever possible. Be adventurous in your fruit choices and make sure your kids are eating a rainbow of fruit choices. That is an easy way to ensure their fruit intake is nutritionally balanced.

Where can you get it?

I like to support local farmers and therefore I try to buy my fresh fruits from the farmers' market or co-op stores that carry organic varieties at reasonable prices.

What kind to buy and how to store it:

Always buy fresh and organic if you can, especially fruits that are likely to be heavily sprayed with pesticides. Ground fruits and low-growing fruits tend to be affected more from the high level of toxicity found in ground water where pesticides are used. Store your fruits in your crisper in the refrigerator and they will last longer and maintain their integrity for a longer period of time. Buying fresh and/or local may not always be realistic, depending on where you live and the season. You can purchase frozen fruit to include in your pops, or better yet, buy or gather an abundance of fruit in season, and freeze it for use at a later date. If you do the latter, however, you should try to use your fresh frozen produce within four to six weeks, as the molecular structure begins to break down and nutritional value begins to decrease.

Pure Sunshine

2 cups chopped strawberries
juice of 1½ Meyer lemons (4 to 5 tablespoons juice)
½ tablespoon chopped fresh mint
4 tablespoons honey
1 cup purified water
1 cup ice

1. Put the strawberries, lemon juice, mint, honey, water, and ice into a blender, and blend all ingredients together into a smooth texture.

2. Pour mixture into chosen pop molds and put sticks in place.

3. Freeze pops until solid.

Makes 6 (4-ounce) pops

Pop Culture Seasonal Tip

Incredibly refreshing, these pops make a perfect summer treat for kids.
Strawberries are juicy and sweet in the summer months and mint grows aplenty!
I like to take these to the beach or the park for a picnic, but
make sure to pack them well in ice before your outing.

Sour Girl

juice of 3 Meyer lemons (½ to ¾ cup juice)
zest of 2 lemons
½ cup raw agave nectar
2 cups purified water

1. Put the lemon juice, lemon zest, agave nectar, and water into a blender, and blend all ingredients together into a smooth texture.

2. Pour mixture into chosen pop molds and put sticks in place.

3. Freeze pops until solid.

Note: If you want to achieve the look of the pop in the photo (opposite), place a very thin slice of lime in your pop mold when the pop is still liquid. Then put your stick in and freeze the pop until solid.

Makes 8 (4-ounce) pops

Pop Culture Shop Tip

Meyer lemons are unique in that they are much sweeter than regular lemons and they make amazing lemonade! They have a smoother skin on the outside than other varieties of lemon. Ask your local grocer if they carry them, and if they do not, check your farmers' market!

Bluebird

½ cup blueberries
½ cup blackberries or boysenberries
1 cup chopped pineapple
2 teaspoons acai powder
4 tablespoons coconut sugar
1 cup purified water

1. Put blueberries, blackberries, pineapple, acai powder, coconut sugar, and water into a blender, and blend all ingredients together into a smooth texture.

2. Pour mixture into chosen pop molds and put sticks in place.

3. Freeze pops until solid.

Makes 8 (4-ounce) pops

Pop Culture Booster Tip

Acai berries were originally found in the Amazon. They contain high levels of antioxidants and are a great immunity booster. You can find the ground powder at your local natural food store.

Island Breeze

5 whole kiwis, peeled and chopped
juice of 1 lime (approximately 2 tablespoons juice)
4 tablespoons honey
1 cup purified water

1. Put kiwis, lime juice, honey, and water into a blender, and blend all ingredients together into a smooth texture.

2. Pour mixture into chosen pop molds and put sticks in place.

3. Freeze pops until solid.

Note: If you want to achieve the look of the pop in the photo (opposite), place a very thin slice of peeled kiwi in your pop mold when the pop is still liquid. Then put your stick in and freeze the pop until solid.

Makes 6 (4-ounce) pops

Pop Culture Seasonal Tip

Kiwifruit is very tart if not fully ripe, so it is good to know when they are at their best. November through May is when kiwifruit is typically in season. Grown in New Zealand, these spectacular fruits have brown furry skin that needs to be peeled off before eating.

Melon Madness

½ honeydew melon, scooped from shell and cut into chunks
1 tablespoon chopped fresh mint
½ tablespoon chopped fresh cilantro
3 tablespoons raw agave nectar
juice of 1 lime (approximately 2 tablespoons juice)
juice of ½ lemon (1½ to 2 tablespoons juice)
1 cup purified water
1 cup ice

1. Put the melon, mint, and cilantro in a blender, and puree until smooth.

2. Add the agave nectar, lime juice, lemon juice, water, and ice, and blend all ingredients together into a smooth texture.

3. Pour mixture into chosen pop molds and put sticks in place.

4. Freeze pops until solid.

Makes 6 (4-ounce) pops

Pop Culture Health Tip

Honeydew melons are very high in vitamin C, so they are great to eat when you are starting to feel a cold coming on or are just a little rundown. They are also low in fat and high in water content, so they're the perfect pleasure on a hot sunny day!

Pomalicious

1 cup pomegranate juice
½ cup raspberries
½ cup cherry tomatoes

1. Combine pomegranate juice, raspberries, and tomatoes in a blender, and puree until smooth.

2. Pour mixture into chosen pop molds and put sticks in place.

3. Freeze pops until solid.

Makes 6 (4-ounce) pops

Pop Culture Health Tip

This powerhouse pop is extremely high in antioxidants and vitamin C and is super refreshing. If your child does not like tomatoes, this is a great way to get those in and boost his or her vitamin C content as well.

Orange Joy

2 cups freshly squeezed orange juice (approximately 6 medium oranges)
1 whole pineapple, skinned, cored, and cut into pieces
3 tablespoons wheat germ
½ cup water

1. Combine orange juice and pineapple in blender, and puree.

2. Add wheat germ and water, and blend all ingredients together into a smooth texture.

3. Pour mixture into chosen pop molds and put sticks in place.

4. Freeze pops until solid.

Makes 8 (4-ounce) pops

Pop Culture Health Tip

Wheat germ is very high in protein — more than most meat products (2) — so it's a great booster to add to lots of your kids' meals, like oatmeal, French toast, smoothies, or even pasta. Many kids enjoy its somewhat nutty flavor.

Refresher

4 cups chopped ripe seedless watermelon
1 cup chopped pineapple
juice of ½ lemon (1½ to 2 tablespoons juice)
3 tablespoons honey

1. Combine watermelon and pineapple in blender, and puree.
2. Add lemon juice and honey, and blend all ingredients together into a smooth texture.
3. Pour mixture into chosen pop molds and put sticks in place.
4. Freeze pops until solid.

Makes 8 (4-ounce) pops

Pop Culture Seasonal Tip

Watermelon is a summer fruit and a great addition to any backyard picnic. Eating watermelon is like having your multivitamin for the day. It also replenishes your body with its high water content.

Veggie Pops

*Putting vegetables in ice pops is not as radical as it may sound.
Don't skip this chapter because you assume you cannot entice
your kids to eat frozen vegetables on a stick — they are really
a lot more delicious than that! The right combination of
vegetables, fruit, and other tasty and healthy ingredients
can make a perfect, refreshing treat.*

Veggie Basics:

When using vegetables in your popsicles, it is important to choose varieties that are in season and fresh. Eating seasonally also helps to naturally keep your body in balance and makes a big difference in the quality of the taste and the nutritional value.

Where can you get it?

Although you can buy most veggies that you will use to create your pops from your favorite grocer, I like to support local growers by buying from them directly at farmers' markets.

What kind to buy and how to store it:

You also want to make sure to buy organic, not conventionally grown vegetables, whenever possible. Read labels carefully so that you know what you are buying. With food being so expensive, it's important to maintain our food as long as possible without wasting it. Don't wash your vegetables before storing them. Veggies stored wet in the refrigerator have increased bacterial growth opportunities, so dry vegetables stay fresh longer. Store dry leafy greens in plastic bags in the refrigerator to help them maintain their natural moisture. Remove green, leafy tops from root vegetables (such as carrots) before storing them in the refrigerator.

Yellow Goodness

1 yellow squash
½ cantaloupe, scooped from shell and cut into chunks
1 cup chopped mango
2 cups sparkling water (any flavor)
¼ cup raw agave nectar

1. Peel yellow squash, cut into rounds, and put into blender. Add chopped cantaloupe, mango, and sparkling water, and blend into a smooth texture.

2. Add agave nectar and blend a second time.

3. Pour mixture into chosen pop molds and put sticks in place.

4. Freeze pops until solid.

Makes 8 (4-ounce) pops

Pop Culture Health Tip

You can feel great about giving your kids cantaloupe. One serving of this orange fruit provides more than 400 percent of their daily vitamin A, and nearly 100 percent of their daily vitamin C! (3)

Green Machine

1 cup chopped raw spinach

2 bananas

1 whole pineapple, peeled, cored, and chopped

2 teaspoons flaxseed

2 cups purified water

1. Combine spinach, bananas, and pineapple in blender and puree.

2. Add flaxseeds and water and puree a second time.

3. Pour mixture into chosen pop molds and put sticks in place.

4. Freeze pops until solid.

Makes 8 (4-ounce) pops

Pop Culture Shop Tip

If your child is a picky eater, this is a great pop for them to try. The Green Machine pop will help him or her eat more veggies and you will feel good about letting him or her have it. If possible, have your child help you grow your own spinach and let him or her harvest it when it's ready to be added into your pops. This will help your child get excited about eating his or her veggies!

Rockstar *with Strawberry Agave Jam*

1 cup chopped strawberries

3 tablespoons raw agave nectar

1 cup chopped raw kale

½ cup blueberries

2 bananas

1 cup purified water

1 tablespoon wheat germ

1. In a small pot over medium heat, combine strawberries and agave nectar, and let simmer until the strawberries resemble a chunky liquid, like jam.

2. Pour a small amount of the jam into the bottom of your chosen pop molds. Let them harden at room temperature, which should take around 15 minutes.

3. Meanwhile, combine kale, blueberries, bananas, water, and wheat germ in a blender, and puree until smooth.

4. When the jam hardens, pour in the kale mixture to fill the molds. Put sticks in place.

5. Freeze pops until solid.

Makes 4 (5-ounce) pops

Pop Culture Clever Idea

You can make the agave jam with any kind of fruit you like. Save any remaining jam to use on toast, sandwiches, or as a general sweet spread on other foods.

Peace Pop

3 carrots, peeled and cut into chunks
1 cup chopped strawberries
1 whole mango, peeled and chopped
¾ cup coconut sugar
1 cup purified water

1. In a steamer pot, boil 4 cups of water. Steam the carrots for 12 minutes. Put the steamed carrots in the blender and puree until smooth.

2. Add strawberries to carrot puree and blend.

3. Add mango, coconut sugar, and water to blended mixture, and blend all ingredients together into a smooth texture.

4. Pour mixture into chosen pop molds and put sticks in place.

5. Freeze pops until solid.

Makes 8 (4-ounce) pops

Pop Culture Baby

If you have a baby, you can save a little of the carrot puree for a fresh snack for your little one, or reserve some for a sweet alternative ingredient for a cupcake recipe.

Harvest Pops

1½ medium apples (for about ½ cup fresh apple puree)
¼ butternut squash (for about 1 cup squash puree)
¼ cup dried cranberries
juice of ½ lemon (1½ to 2 tablespoons juice)
juice of 1 orange (approximately ⅓ cup juice)
1 teaspoon wheat germ
3 tablespoons honey
1 cup purified water

1. Peel apples and cut into chunks.

2. Peel butternut squash and cut into chunks.

3. In a steamer pot, boil 4 cups of water. Steam the apples and butternut squash for 12 minutes, or until soft.

4. Put the steamed apples and butternut squash in a blender, and puree until smooth.

5. Add the dried cranberries, lemon juice, orange juice, wheat germ, honey, and water. Blend until smooth. (Note: If the mixture is too thick, add some more water.)

6. Pour mixture into chosen pop molds and put sticks in place. Freeze pops until solid.

Makes 8 (3-ounce) pops

Pop Culture Clever Tip

Make a little extra of the puree mixture and turn it into a soup! Add 3 cups of the apple—butternut squash puree to 1 quart of chicken stock and 2 tablespoons fresh tarragon. Mix together with salt & pepper and let simmer for about 12 minutes. Serve warm with fresh bread and a little Parmesan cheese grated on top.

Cool-n-Fresh

1 whole cucumber, peeled and chopped
1 cup chopped fresh pineapple
juice of ½ lemon (1½ to 2 tablespoons juice)
1 whole zucchini, peeled and chopped
3 tablespoons coconut sugar
½ cup water

1. Combine cucumber, pineapple, lemon juice, and zucchini in a blender, and puree until smooth.

2. Add coconut sugar and water and puree for a second time.

3. Pour mixture into chosen pop molds and put sticks in place.

4. Freeze pops until solid.

Makes 8 (4-ounce) pops

Pop Culture Clever Tip

You can use any extra cucumber, pineapple, and lemon to make a refreshing drink for your family. Add them to a pitcher of water with some agave nectar for a nice summer drink.

Yogurt Pops

Most kids love yogurt, but they are used to the sugar-filled varieties sold at most grocery stores. The pops in this chapter offer delicious natural flavors without the high sugar price tag. Your kids will love them, and you can feel good about serving them as snacks.

Yogurt Basics:

Yogurt is an amazing food that is high in protein. Good-quality yogurts contain live active bacteria, which are great for your digestive tract and may even extend your life. (4) It is a great source of calcium and phosphorus and is particularly good for the growing bones of children.

Where can you get it?

These pops are all made from plain yogurts of varieties that can be bought at your local grocer. Good-quality live bacteria yogurt may have to be bought in your local health food store, but it is becoming more common in most supermarkets.

What kind to buy and how to store it:

There are many kinds of yogurts and all of the plain varieties are good for you, but some have more proteins than others. There are many brands of yogurt, even organic ones, that offer flavored yogurt varieties, but they often contain high levels of sugars. In my book *Organically Raised,* I offer a variety of fruit yogurt recipes that contain no sugar, but taste great! Try making a fruit puree and mixing it into a plain yogurt for a healthy snack for you and your children.

Always store your yogurt in your refrigerator. Because I don't like the taste that some plastic containers give food, I like to take it out of the plastic container and put it in a glass jar with a sealable lid.

Whole-fat yogurt has its full fat content, which particularly benefits babies as their brains are developing.

Low-fat yogurt has had about 3 grams of fat removed per serving.

Live-bacteria yogurt is easier for folks to digest, is great as a protein-rich food, and is a great "growing food" for kids.

Greek yogurt is a creamier variety than other yogurts and contains less cow milkfat.

Pink Princess

2 cups chopped strawberries

2 bananas

juice of ½ lemon (1½ to 2 tablespoons juice)

2 tablespoons honey or raw agave nectar

1 cup plain Greek yogurt

1. Blend strawberries and bananas together in a blender.
2. Add lemon juice, honey, and yogurt, and blend all ingredients together into a smooth texture.
3. Pour mixture into chosen pop molds and put sticks in place.
4. Freeze pops until solid.

Makes 6 (4-ounce) pops

Pop Culture Tip

Greek yogurt is becoming more popular. That's because it has about double the protein that regular yogurt has and it's high in probiotics and low in carbs! (5)

Beach Day

2 bananas
½ cup chopped almonds
2 tablespoons wheat germ
3 tablespoons honey
½ cup kefir
½ cup plain yogurt

1. Blend bananas, almonds, and wheat germ together in a blender.

2. Add honey, kefir, and yogurt, and blend all ingredients together into a smooth texture.

3. Pour mixture into chosen pop molds and put sticks in place.

4. Freeze pops until solid.

Makes 6 (4-ounce) pops

Pop Culture Health Tip

Kefir is similar to yogurt, and also contains an active bacteria in it that our bodies need. It has probiotics, which are great for the digestive tract. Big companies have jumped on the kefir bandwagon and now sell this super healthy drink at standard grocery markets.

Blackberry Swirl

1 ½ cups blackberries
juice of ½ lemon (1 ½ to 2 tablespoons juice)
1 banana
4 tablespoons raw agave nectar
½ cup plain Greek yogurt

1. Combine blackberries and lemon juice in a blender. Add banana, agave nectar, and yogurt, and puree until smooth.

2. Pour mixture into chosen pop molds and put sticks in place.

3. Freeze pops until solid.

Note: For fun, add a couple of whole blackberries to each ice pop mold, creating a surprise flavor burst when the pops are eaten.

Makes 6 (4-ounce) pops

Pop Culture Seasonal Tip

Blackberries are at their best during the summer months. I like to take my kids to U-pick farms during the summer months and come home with freshly picked berries for pops and pies!

Goo Goo Ga Ga

1 medium apple, peeled and cut into chunks (1½ cups)
1½ cups mango chunks, either fresh or frozen
½ cup plain Greek yogurt

1. Over boiling water in a steamer pot, place apples and mangoes in basket. Steam for about 15 minutes or until soft.

2. Place steamed apples and mangoes into a blender and puree.

3. Add yogurt and blend all ingredients together to a smooth texture.

4. Freeze pops until solid.

Makes 6 (4-ounce) pops

Pop Culture Toddler Tip

I have a toddler and I know how much of the day is on the go. It's tough to get him to sit with us and to enjoy a leisurely meal. Snacks need to be quick and need to contain proteins for him to keep going. My toddler likes this pop and I can serve it to him and a buddy when they are running around outside. I keep these on hand for an easy, healthy snack that all the toddlers love.

Ice Pops for Breakfast

¾ cup almond butter

3 bananas

3 tablespoons chopped walnuts

½ tablespoon wheat germ

1 cup plain yogurt

I. Combine almond butter and bananas in blender and puree.

2. Add walnuts, wheat germ, and yogurt, and blend well.

3. Pour mixture into chosen pop molds and put sticks in place.

4. Freeze pops until solid.

Makes 4 (5-ounce) pops

Pop Culture Baby

This is a great pop for baby, especially if they tend to be a bit picky in their eating.
Try it for breakfast for the whole family on a hot summer morning.

Green Wonder

¼ cup unsweetened coconut flakes
¼ cup chopped pistachios
½ cup coconut milk
1 teaspoon vanilla extract
1 tablespoon wheat germ
3 tablespoons coconut sugar
½ cup plain yogurt

1. Combine coconut flakes and pistachios in a blender and blend.
2. Add coconut milk, vanilla, wheat germ, coconut sugar, and yogurt, and puree until smooth.
3. Pour mixture into chosen pop molds and put sticks in place.
4. Freeze pops until solid.

Makes 8 (4-ounce) pops

Pop Culture Ingredient Tip

Coconut is a unique ingredient with a special flavor that immediately takes you to the tropics. The truth is coconut, in its many forms of milk, flakes, and water, does more for you than bring on beachy dreams. It is an excellent source of saturated fats, which help boost your immune system.

Peach Party

2 cups chopped peaches (4 medium peaches)
1 cup chopped pineapple
½ cup chopped mango
juice of ½ lemon (1½ to 2 tablespoons juice)
¼ cup raw agave nectar
1 cup Greek yogurt

I. Combine peaches, pineapple, and mango in blender, and blend.

2. Add lemon juice, agave nectar, and yogurt, and puree until smooth.

3. Pour mixture into chosen pop molds and put sticks in place.

4. Freeze pops until solid.

Makes 8 (4-ounce) pops

Pop Culture Seasonal Tip

Everyone knows that a ripe, sweet peach comes only once a year, in the summer! It's a beautiful juicy fruit that can be turned into jam, pie, agave syrup, cakes, salsa, and of course, ice pops! This is a pretty pop that everyone loves, and it tastes so sweet you cannot believe there is no refined sugar in it!

Citrus Cooler

2 cups fresh-squeezed orange juice (approximately 6 oranges)
1 cup chopped pineapple
juice of ½ lemon (approximately 1½ to 2 tablespoons juice)
2 tablespoons raw agave nectar
½ cup yogurt (any variety)

1. Combine orange juice and pineapple in a blender and mix together.

2. Add lemon juice, agave nectar, and yogurt, and puree until smooth.

3. Pour mixture into chosen pop molds and put sticks in place.

4. Freeze pops until solid.

Makes 8 (4-ounce) pops

Pop Culture Seasonal Tip

This is a vitamin C—packed pop! If you want to boost your immune system, this is the one to make. If you feel a cold coming on, you may also want to include actual vitamin C tablets in the pop to give yourself an extra boost to ward off a summer cold.

Tofu Pops

Tofu gives an added boost of protein to your pops for those kids who may struggle with eating meat or other forms of proteins. It's also a nice ingredient to use because it takes on flavors easily. Even kids who think they don't like tofu will have a change of heart!

Tofu Basics:

Tofu is made from soya beans and is entirely plant-based. It's an amazing source of protein, which is why it's an ideal food for vegans and vegetarians. Tofu is one of the only food products that provide all nine essential amino acids. It contains no animal fats or cholesterol, is low in sodium, contains few calories, and is easy to digest. It is also an excellent source of iron and vitamin B. And because calcium sulfate is used in the manufacturing process, it is a worthwhile source of calcium.(6)

Where can you get it?

Tofu has become very popular in recent years and is now available in almost all grocery stores. It is sold in the refrigerated section of the store and is usually located with the "healthy" stuff.

What kind to buy and how to store it:

Tofu is sold packed in water and comes in varieties of silken, soft, firm, and extra-firm. For making popsicles, choose silken, as it is soft and easy to blend. The firm varieties are better for grilling or creating meals with. After you open the package, make sure to rinse the tofu with water, take out as much as you will need, and restore the rest in water in either a stainless steel container or a BPA-free plastic container.

Classic Vanilla Tofu

2 tablespoons vanilla extract
4 tablespoons honey
freshly grated nutmeg (just a little pinch)
black pepper (just a little pinch)
⅓ cup heavy cream
1 cup unsweetened coconut milk
½ cup silken tofu

I. In a bowl, combine the vanilla, honey, nutmeg, black pepper, heavy cream, coconut milk, and tofu. Let sit for 5 minutes to infuse flavors.

2. Put mixture into a blender, and puree until smooth.

3. Pour mixture into chosen pop molds and put sticks in place.

4. Freeze pops until solid.

Note: Please remember that it is not safe to give honey to children under the age of one.

Makes 8 (4-ounce) pops

Pop Culture Fun Fact

The black pepper in this recipe gives just a little punch that makes the pop a bit more savory and brings out the sweetness of the other ingredients. Just a pinch goes a long way.

Purple Fantastic Tofu

4 cups water

2 pears, peeled, cored, and chopped

½ cup blueberries

⅓ cup raisins

¾ cup silken tofu

4 tablespoons raw agave nectar

1. In a steamer pot, boil 4 cups of water. Place the chopped pears in the steamer basket and steam for about 8 minutes or until soft. (If your pears are soft and ripe, there is no need to steam them.)

2. Add steamed pears, blueberries, raisins, tofu, and agave nectar to blender, and puree until smooth.

3. Pour mixture into chosen pop molds and put sticks in place.

4. Freeze pops until solid.

Note: To get the layered effect shown in photograph, pour half of the complete mixture in all your molds first and let freeze. Then add a layer of plain pureed blueberries on top of the frozen original mixture, and let that freeze. Repeat the layers until your pops are frozen to the top.

Makes 8 (4-ounce) pops

Pop Culture Baby

This recipe is also good as a baby food! Leave out the agave nectar and don't freeze. Serve to babies 9 + months.

Summer Splash Tofu

juice of 1½ whole oranges (approximately ½ cup juice)
1 cup chopped strawberries
½ cup blueberries
1 teaspoon flaxseed
¾ cup silken tofu
3 tablespoons dark honey

1. Combine orange juice, strawberries, blueberries, flaxseed, tofu, and honey in blender, and puree until smooth.

2. Pour mixture into chosen pop molds and put sticks in place.

3. Freeze pops until solid.

Makes 8 (4-ounce) pops

Pop Culture Health Tip

Flaxseed has high amounts of fiber, antioxidants, and Omega-3 fatty acids, and is considered very good for you. A little goes a long way!

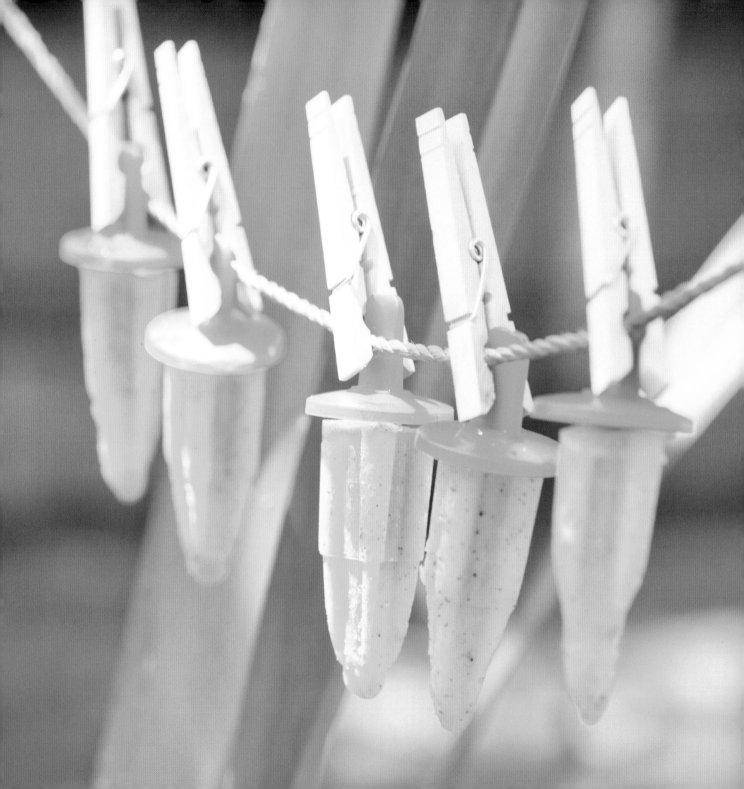

Tropical Tofu

juice of 2 oranges (approximately ⅔ cup juice)
3 kiwis, peeled and chopped
2 mangoes, peeled and chopped
1 (8.5-ounce) container O.N.E. Coconut Water with a Splash of Passion Fruit
¼ cup silken tofu
3 tablespoons coconut sugar

1. Combine orange juice, kiwis, mangoes, coconut water, tofu, and coconut sugar in your blender, and puree until smooth.

2. Pour mixture into chosen pop molds and put sticks in place.

3. Freeze pops until solid.

Makes 8 (5-ounce) pops

Pop Culture Health Tip

Coconut water is the purest liquid, second only to water. It is chock-full of electrolytes, calcium, potassium, and magnesium (7). I like the O.N.E. Coconut Water brand because it is tasty, healthy, and comes in fun flavors. If you cannot find this brand at your local store, you can use plain coconut juice and flavor it with a passion fruit juice of your liking.

Pistachio Tofu Pop

⅓ cup silken tofu

3 cups whole milk

1 cup ground pistachios

1 teaspoon cardamom

4 tablespoons raw agave nectar

1 banana

1. In a pot over medium heat, combine tofu and milk and bring to a boil. Reduce heat, add ground pistachios and cardamom, and simmer for 5 minutes, stirring occasionally to prevent burning. Remove from heat and let cool briefly.

2. Transfer mixture to a blender and add agave nectar and banana. Puree all ingredients until smooth.

3. Pour mixture into chosen pop molds and put sticks in place.

4. Freeze pops until solid.

Makes 8 (4-ounce) pops

Pop Culture Prep Tip

Pistachios, and all nuts and seeds, can easily be ground up in a coffee grinder. Just put the nuts in, press the top, and it's done in about 30 seconds!

Bing Cherry Tofu Pop

⅓ cup silken tofu

2 cups pitted, fresh Bing cherries (or frozen cherries)

2 cups fresh-squeezed orange juice (from approximately 6 oranges)

¼ cup raw agave nectar

1 teaspoon wheat germ

1. Combine tofu, cherries, and orange juice in blender, and puree to desired smoothness.

2. Add agave nectar and wheat germ and mix. Puree until smooth.

3. Pour mixture into chosen pop molds and put sticks in place.

4. Freeze pops until solid.

Makes 6 (4-ounce) pops

Pop Culture Shop Tip

Bing cherries are amazingly sweet when in season. They usually are best in early June through July and have a really short seasonal life. Remember, the darker the cherry, the sweeter the taste.

For Toddler Tofu

½ cup silken tofu

2 bananas

½ cup chopped dates

1. Combine tofu, bananas, and dates together in blender and puree to desired smoothness.

2. Pour mixture into chosen pop molds and put sticks in place.

3. Freeze pops until solid.

Makes 6 (4-ounce) pops

Pop Culture Health Tip

Dates have many restorative qualities for children and adults and can help with digestion. Dates soaked in warm milk make a good drink for a child with digestive issues.

Herbal Tea Pops

Whether to soothe a teething toddler or calm yourself after a wild day, herbal tea pops can be healthy and refreshing and can create the perfect sensation right when it's needed.

Herbal Tea Basics:

Herbal teas are not really teas at all, but more like flower drinks. They contain no caffeine and are well known to hold many medicinal properties. The trick to making these pops taste great is letting the teas have time to infuse. You want to give each tea mixture plenty of time to simmer so that the flavors blend together well and so you extract the most medicinal properties as possible.

Where can you get it?

Herbals teas are available at almost any grocer these days, but to get the good stuff — the fresh loose tea varieties — it's well worth it to go to a tea shop or order online. Living in Los Angeles provides me with the opportunity to go to special tea stores like the Chado Tea Room. If you live in New York you can check out The Tea Spot or Radiance Tea House & Books. It's a lot of fun to go to a teahouse and you may want to check your area to see if you have one close by to help inspire you. Please check the Resources section for my favorite online stores as well.

What kind to buy and how to store it:

There are so many varieties of herbal teas and I have made a short list of the most popular ones and their medicinal properties, so you can play with making different pops to suit your needs. Store your teas in a wooden bowl or basket in a dry area.

Acai Berry: antioxidant; boosts immunity

Chamomile: calming; soothes sore throats

Echinacea: boosts immunity

Ginger: soothes upset stomach

Goldenseal: aids digestion

Kava Kava: reduces anxiety

Lavender: soothes tummy aches and calms nerves

Lemongrass: has antibiotic properties

Mint: good for tummy aches

Raspberry Leaf: alleviates cramping and is a tonic

Rooibos: antioxidant; boosts immunity

Sore Throat Soother

4 cups water

4 chamomile tea bags

4 tablespoons honey

I. Bring water to a boil on the stovetop. Add tea bags and honey and simmer for 10 minutes. Remove pan from heat and let tea cool to lukewarm.

2. Pour mixture into chosen pop molds and put sticks in place.

3. Freeze pops until solid.

Note: Please remember that it is not safe to give honey to children under the age of one.

Makes 8 (4-ounce) pops

Pop Culture Tea Tip

Chamomile is well-known for its amazing soothing qualities. It is good for babies with colic, is an instant healer for a sore throat, and is a wonderful relaxing treat while in the bath. These tea pops are refreshingly light, surprisingly tasty, and great for a summer treat.

Kava Calm

4 cups water
2 kava kava tea bags
2 spearmint tea bags
1 drop vanilla extract
¼ cup honey

1. Bring water to a boil on the stovetop. Add tea bags, vanilla, and honey and simmer for 10 minutes. Remove pan from heat and let tea cool to lukewarm.

2. Pour mixture into chosen pop molds and put sticks in place.

3. Freeze pops until solid.

Note: Please remember that it is not safe to give honey to children under the age of one.

Makes 8 (4-ounce) pops

Pop Culture Health Tip

Kava Kava is well-known to reduce anxiety, so if you or your child has high stress, this tea is for you. This is a gentle tea mixture that tastes great and is a real treat when frozen into an ice pop.

Happy Tummy Tea Pop

4 cups water

2 mint tea bags

2 chamomile tea bags

1 ginger tea bag

2 fresh lavender tea bags

¼ cup raw agave nectar

juice of ½ lemon (1½ to 2 tablespoons juice)

½ cup ice

1. Bring water to a boil on the stovetop. Add all tea bags and agave nectar and simmer for 10 minutes. Remove pan from heat and let tea cool to lukewarm.

2. Pour tea mixture into blender. Add lemon juice and ice and blend to a smooth texture.

3. Freeze pops until solid.

Note: If you cannot find fresh lavender tea bags, you can make your own by harvesting approximately 2 ounces of lavender flowers and tying them up in a muslin bag.

Makes 8 (4-ounce) pops

Pop Culture Clever Tip

Herbal tea flowers are easy to grow, and they make lovely fresh flower arrangements. Herbal teas are really just flowers and not technically tea at all because there is no caffeine in them. Try growing your own chamomile, mint, and lavender, and creating some of your own tea mixtures.

Rooibos Red Tea Immunity Pops

4 cups water

3 rooibos red tea bags

¼ cup honey

juice of 1 whole grapefruit (approximately ⅔ cup juice)

1 cup chopped strawberries

juice of ½ lemon (1½ to 2 tablespoons juice)

1 cup ice

1. Bring water to a boil on the stovetop. Add tea bags and honey and simmer on low for 10 minutes. Remove pan from heat and let tea cool to lukewarm.

2. Pour tea mixture into blender. Add grapefruit juice, strawberries, lemon juice, and ice, and blend to a smooth texture.

3. Pour mixture into chosen pop molds and put sticks in place.

4. Freeze pops until solid.

Makes 8 (4-ounce) pops

Pop Culture Health Tip

Rooibos is a very high antioxidant tea that really boosts your immune system. It is an herbal tea, which means there is no caffeine and it is completely natural. Rooibos tea is completely pure, as it contains no additives, preservatives, or colorants. (8) These pops taste amazing and are my son Zoë's favorite.

Tea Party Pops

4 cups water

2 raspberry leaf tea bags

2 lemongrass tea bags

1 spearmint tea bag

1 rose petal muslin bag (handmade)

1 cinnamon stick

¼ cup honey

juice of 1 whole lemon (approximately 3 tablespoons juice)

1. Bring water to a boil on the stovetop. Add all tea bags, the cinnamon stick, and honey, and simmer on low for 10 minutes.

2. Add lemon juice, then remove pan from heat and let tea cool to lukewarm.

3. Pour mixture into chosen pop molds and put sticks in place.

4. Freeze pops until solid.

Note: For the rose petals, simply gather a handful of organic rose petals, which you get from a natural grower, your own organic garden, or online, and place them in a muslin bag. Tie off bag with twine and you're ready to steep the tea.

Makes 10 (3-ounce) pops

Pop Culture Party Tip

My daughter Lotus loves these pops to serve to her friends. They taste great and are fun to have around for impromptu tea parties. I like to use daintier molds to keep with the delicate theme of the occasion.

Chocolate Pops

Just because there is chocolate in these pops, doesn't mean they're not healthy. If you choose the chocolate carefully, you can make pops with incredible depth of flavor without all the hidden refined sugar. Your family will love these pops, and you will feel good about offering this awesome snack.

Chocolate Basics:

My son Bodhi LOVES chocolate, so this section is really dedicated to him. He told me once that he wanted to pick chocolate off a tree like a flower, and even though he did not know it, he was right about where it comes from. Chocolate really does grow on trees, the "cocoa" tree, and is mostly harvested in Africa. The pods are football-shaped and grow not only from the branches, but also from the tree truck itself! (9)

When making chocolate treats for your family, keep in mind that unless the chocolate is raw and unsweetened, it contains some sugar. So you want to make sure to buy organic varieties as much as possible.

Where can you get it?

Most natural food stores carry all of the various forms of chocolate you may require and you can get good-quality organic varieties there as well. You may need to investigate a little online for raw chocolate choices, but you can even get raw chocolate bars online. Check out the Resources section for some online choices.

What kind to buy & how to store it:

There are many varieties and forms of chocolate: unsweetened, sweetened, dark, white, milk, chips, and cocoa powder and nibs. The specific pop you are creating will determine the variety and form of chocolate you will need. Keep in mind that true chocolate has some caffeine in it, so managing how much your children consume is important. Sweetened chocolate typically has chocolate liquor, sugar, and cocoa butter in it. White chocolate contains no chocolate liquor but does have cocoa butter. Most chocolate around the world is roasted, which removes many of the health benefits. The healthiest form of chocolate is raw organic chocolate. This typically comes in the form of cocoa powder and nibs, which are the least processed and maintain a truer form without roasting. Cocoa powder and cocoa nibs are also available unsweetened. (10)

It's best to store your chocolate in a cool dry place with a temperature range of 60 to 75 degrees Fahrenheit.

Mexican Spiced Fire Pops

4 ounces chopped bittersweet chocolate

½ cup carob chips

½ teaspoon vanilla extract

2 pinches ground cinnamon

2 pinches cayenne pepper

½ cup chopped raw kale

½ cup heavy cream

2 cups whole milk

1. Combine chopped chocolate and carob chips in a double boiler. As the chocolate and carob start to melt together, add the vanilla and cinnamon.

2. When chocolate is fully melted, remove from heat, and pour the warm mixture into blender. Add the cayenne, kale, heavy cream, and whole milk, and blend all ingredients together into a smooth texture. (Make sure the kale is fully processed in the mixture.)

3. Pour mixture into chosen pop molds and put sticks in place.

4. Freeze pops until solid.

Makes 8 (4-ounce) pops

Pop Culture Clever Tip

If you don't have a double boiler, you can use a cooking pot and metal bowl to melt the chocolate. Put about 2 cups of water in the pot and bring to a boil. Place the metal bowl, filled with your chocolate pieces, on top of the boiling water, and that's that! The chocolate will melt quickly, so make sure to have all of your other ingredients ready to go!

Soy Joy

8 ounces chopped dark chocolate
1 tablespoon chopped fresh mint leaves
1 teaspoon mint extract
1 tablespoon flaxseed
½ cup heavy cream
1½ cups plain soy milk

1. Melt the chocolate in a double boiler. As the chocolate starts to melt, add the chopped mint leaves and mint extract, and stir to combine.

2. When chocolate is fully melted, remove from heat, and pour mixture into a blender. Add flaxseed, heavy cream, and soy milk to the blender, and blend all ingredients together into a smooth texture.

3. Pour mixture into chosen pop molds and put sticks in place.

4. Freeze pops until solid.

Makes 8 (4-ounce) pops

Pop Culture Shop Tip

You can buy natural organic mint extract online and use it for a
variety of recipes. I also like to take fresh mint leaves
and add them to my raw sugar to make mint-flavored sugar.

Heavenly

8 ounces chopped white chocolate
2 cups unsweetened coconut milk
1 teaspoon wheat germ
3 tablespoons raw agave nectar
½ cup chopped walnuts

1. Melt white chocolate pieces in the top of a double boiler. As the chocolate starts to melt, add the coconut milk and stir to combine.

2. When chocolate and coconut milk are melted together, remove from heat, and pour mixture into a blender. Add the wheat germ, agave nectar, and chopped walnuts to the blender with the chocolate. Let cool to room temperature.

3. Blend all ingredients together into a smooth texture.

4. Pour mixture into chosen pop molds and put sticks in place.

5. Freeze pops until solid.

Note: Keep a few extra chopped walnuts aside to drop into the top of the mold before pouring the mixture on top. You'll end up with some nuts at the tip of the pop.

Makes 6 (4-ounce) pops

Pop Culture Fun Fact

While white chocolate is not considered real chocolate, it does contain cocoa butter, which comes from the cocoa bean, from which real chocolate is made.

Choco-Berry Pops

¾ cup milk chocolate chips, melted
½ cup cocoa powder
½ cup raspberries
½ cup chopped strawberries
1 cup whole milk
1 cup vanilla rice milk

1. Melt the chocolate chips in the top of a double boiler. When chocolate is melted, add the cocoa powder and stir to combine. Remove from heat, and pour mixture into a blender.

2. Add raspberries, strawberries, whole milk, and rice milk to blender with the chocolate. Blend all ingredients together into a smooth texture.

3. Pour mixture into chosen pop molds and put sticks in place.

4. Freeze pops until solid.

Makes 6 (4-ounce) pops

Pop Culture Shop Tip

You can often buy both natural and organic chocolate chips and cocoa powder at your local natural foods store. You can also turn your cocoa powder into an amazing hot cocoa drink in the winter, by combining 1 cup cocoa powder, 1 cup milk, and ½ cup cream in a pan on a stovetop; stir until well mixed; and let it get nice and hot. Serve with a nice scoop of agave whipped cream on top (1 cup heavy whipping cream and ½ cup agave; beat with a mixer until fluffy).

Peanut Butter & Chocolate Classic

¼ cup semisweet chocolate chips, melted
¼ cup organic peanut butter
1 tablespoon wheat germ
2 bananas
1 cup soy milk

1. Melt the chocolate chips in the top of a double boiler. When chocolate is melted, pour it into a blender, add peanut butter, and blend.

2. Add wheat germ, bananas, and milk to the chocolate–peanut butter mixture and blend all ingredients together into a smooth texture.

3. Pour mixture into chosen pop molds and put sticks in place.

4. Freeze pops until solid.

Makes 8 (4-ounce) pops

Pop Culture Shop Tip

Try almond butter as an alternative to peanut butter. You can get it at almost any grocer now, and it's usually sold right next to the peanut butter. You can also try this recipe with different types of chocolate.

Happiness

1 cup milk
1 cup heavy cream
5 ounces chopped white chocolate
2 drops natural peppermint extract
2 tablespoons raw agave nectar
½ cup cold milk

1. Combine 1 cup milk and heavy cream in a pot over medium heat. Heat gently for 4 minutes, then turn heat down to low to keep warm.

2. Melt the white chocolate in the top of a double boiler. Once melted, pour the chocolate into a blender and add the warm milk mixture.

3. Add peppermint extract, agave nectar, and cold milk to blender, and blend all ingredients together into a smooth texture.

4. Pour mixture into chosen pop molds and put sticks in place.

5. Freeze pops until solid.

Makes 8 (4-ounce) pops

Pop Culture Party Tip

Try these for a party treat instead of traditional cupcakes or sheet cake. Be the one to start the popsicle trend in your group of friends. Let your friends know that ice pops are the new cupcakes!

Vincent's Chocolate Wonder

8 ounces chopped dark chocolate
2 cups whole milk
3 tablespoons chopped almonds, plus extra for texture
1 tablespoon flaxseed

1. Melt the dark chocolate in the top of a double boiler. Once melted, pour chocolate into blender and add milk, 3 tablespoons chopped almonds, and flaxseed. Blend all ingredients together into a smooth texture.

2. Add extra chopped almonds for crunch; stir, but do not blend.

3. Pour mixture into chosen pop molds and put sticks in place.

4. Freeze pops until solid.

Makes 8 (4-ounce) pops

Pop Culture Health Tip

Dark chocolate has many health benefits: it can lower blood pressure, is a potent antioxidant, and is good for your heart! (11) So if you are a chocolate fan and health-conscious, this is the perfect choice for you.

Little Dippers

vanilla soy milk

chocolate soy milk

1. Choose your pop mold. Pour in a little vanilla soy milk. Let it semi-freeze and add a stick to each pop once the base of the pop is solid enough to hold it upright.

2. After the bottom layer is completely frozen, pour in a second layer using chocolate soy milk. Let the second layer freeze completely.

3. Repeat steps until the mold is full and all layers are frozen solid.

Makes 10 (3-ounce) pops

Pop Culture Health Tip

Soy is an amazing source of protein and this frozen treat is great for teething toddlers. They will enjoy it while getting in a healthy dose of their daily nutrition.

Specialty Pops

The pops in this chapter each contain unusual ingredients that you might not expect to find in your average ice pop. Often savory ingredients can make for a delightful surprise when married with carefully chosen ingredients in an ice pop.

Specialty basics:

These creative pops contain foods such as like balsamic vinegar, mascarpone cheese, lavender, quinoa, and red beans. Practically any foods can be used in pops, if mixed with the right ingredients, the combinations will result in delicious, healthy, and fresh treats.

Where can you get special ingredients?

When you are cooking with special ingredients, you may have to buy them at more specialized stores or online. I have included resources in the back of this book for where to purchase certain specialty items for these pops, but what is fun is exploring your own city to find stores that carry unique ingredients that you may have never known existed before.

What to buy and how to store it:

When it comes to any ingredients — but particularly those specialty ones that you go the extra mile for — buy fresh, high-quality, organic (when you can) products. Using the best-quality ingredients can make a big difference in flavor and will really elevate these unique pops to treats for special occasions.

Granola Goodness

1 cup rice milk
2 bananas
1 cup vanilla-flavored granola
1 teaspoon wheat germ

1. Combine rice milk, bananas, granola, and wheat germ in a blender, and puree to a smooth texture.

2. Pour mixture into chosen pop molds and put sticks in place.

3. Freeze pops until solid.

Makes 5 (4-ounce) pops

Pop Culture Shop Tip

You will likely find various kinds of granola in the bulk-bin section of your local natural food store. There are often many flavors of granola to choose from. The Granola Goodness pop is simple and flexible, so substitute your favorite kind of granola for the vanilla-flavored granola suggested above. It will alter the taste, but will still keep the nutrient value.

Treehouse Pop

¼ cup ground almonds
¼ cup ground cashews
¼ cup ground walnuts
¼ cup peanut butter
1 banana
½ cup heavy cream
½ cup milk

1. Combine all ground nuts and peanut butter into the blender and puree.

2. Add the banana, heavy cream, and milk, and blend all ingredients together to a smooth texture.

3. Pour mixture into chosen pop molds and put sticks in place.

4. Freeze pops until solid.

Makes 8 (4-ounce) pops

Pop Culture Health Tip

This pop is very high in protein, so it is especially good for vegetarian families. My son Zoë has been a vegetarian his whole life. I am always looking for protein alternatives for him, and these pops are perfect!

Spicy Italian

2 ½ cups chopped strawberries
2 tablespoons balsamic vinegar
2 tablespoons chopped walnuts
2 tablespoons unsweetened coconut flakes
½ cup heavy cream
½ cup mascarpone cheese or ricotta

1. Put the strawberries, balsamic vinegar, and chopped walnuts into the blender, and puree.

2. Add the coconut flakes, heavy cream, and mascarpone or ricotta cheese, and blend all ingredients together to desired texture.

3. Pour mixture into chosen pop molds and put sticks in place.

4. Freeze pops until solid.

Makes 8 (4-ounce) pops

Pop Culture Party Tip

These are whimsical-looking pops and they make a great addition to any party menu. For a very decadent frozen treat, make these pops at the same time as the mint chocolate pops called Soy Joy (recipe page 107) and layer the two pop mixtures (as shown in photo opposite).

Piña Colada Surprise

1 whole pineapple, skinned, cored, and cut into pieces
1 cup chopped strawberries
¾ cup coconut milk
2 tablespoons maple raw agave nectar

1. Put the pineapple, strawberries, and coconut milk into a blender, and puree.

2. Add the maple agave nectar and blend all ingredients together to desired texture.

3. Pour mixture into chosen pop molds and put sticks in place.

4. Freeze pops until solid.

Note: To create the two-tone effect shown in the photo (opposite), add a few thinly sliced strawberries to the pop immediately after you pour the liquid in the molds.

Makes 8 (4-ounce) pops

Pop Culture Shop Tip

Maple agave nectar is sold at health food stores or Trader Joe's. It is sold as an alternative to traditional syrup, and we use it on pancakes and waffles in our home. It's delicious and the kids love it. It adds a really nice sweet element to these tropical pops.

Lavender Flower Power

1 tablespoon edible lavender flowers (plus a few extra for garnish)
1 teaspoon lavender extract
4 tablespoons honey
½ cup heavy cream
1½ cups whole milk

1. Combine the lavender flowers, lavender extract, and honey in a large bowl, and mix together.

2. Add the heavy cream and milk, transfer to a blender, and blend all ingredients together to a smooth texture.

3. Pour mixture into chosen pop molds and put sticks in place.

4. Freeze pops until solid.

Note: Add one tiny drop of violet-colored food coloring to make the color really pop! And, to make the pops extra-special, add additional edible lavender flowers to the top of the pop after you pour your mixture in the mold.

Makes 6 (4-ounce) pops

Pop Culture Party Tip

Many folks do not know you can consume lavender, but you can. English lavender is said to be the most popular edible form. The flavor is a subtle and somewhat acquired taste that is really refreshing and soothing. Lavender is an herb that is well known to calm the nerves. Just the tiniest bit of lavender extract goes a long way, so use it sparingly.

Protein Bar

½ cup cooked red kidney beans
1 cup chopped pineapple
1 cup chopped mango
½ cup raisins
1 banana
½ cup chopped pecans
1 cup milk

1. Combine red beans, pineapple, and mango in a blender, and puree.

2. Add raisins, banana, pecans, and milk, and blend all ingredients together to a smooth texture.

3. Pour mixture into chosen pop molds and put sticks in place.

4. Freeze pops until solid.

Makes 6 (4-ounce) pops

Pop Culture Health Tip

Red beans are a great source of fiber and are virtually fat-free and
very high in protein. You cannot really taste the beans in these pops,
but you get the nutritional benefits.

Quinoa Pop

1 cup quinoa
2 cups water
1 cup blueberries
5 tablespoons agave nectar
¼ cup coconut sugar
2 bananas
1 cup yogurt
½ cup milk

1. In a pot, combine the quinoa with the water, cover with a lid, and bring to a boil. Reduce heat to medium and let simmer for about 10 minutes or until the water is absorbed.

2. Transfer quinoa to a blender and add the blueberries, agave nectar, coconut sugar, bananas, yogurt, and milk. Blend all ingredients together to a smooth texture.

3. Pour mixture into chosen pop molds and put sticks in place.

4. Freeze pops until solid.

Makes 8 (4-ounce) pops

Pop Culture Health Tip

Quinoa is a recently rediscovered ancient seed native to South America. The Inca people recognized quinoa's value and documented that it increased the stamina of their warriors. Quinoa is high in protein, and the protein it supplies is complete protein, meaning that it includes all nine essential amino acids. (12) So kids (and grownups), eat your quinoa!

Tween Twister

4 carrots, chopped
1 cup chopped raw spinach
1 cup chopped pineapple
1 cup pomegranate juice
juice of ½ orange (approximately 3 tablespoons juice)

1. In a steamer pot, place carrots in basket and steam for about 15 minutes or until soft. Place steamed carrots in a blender and puree.

2. Add spinach, pineapple, pomegranate juice, and orange juice, and blend all ingredients together to a smooth texture.

3. Pour mixture into chosen pop molds and put sticks in place.

4. Freeze pops until solid.

Makes 6 (4-ounce) pops

Pop Culture Picky Eater Tip

This pop is obviously packed full of nutrient-rich foods, so if your child is a picky eater, try this pop. It tastes great and you are getting in all the fruits and veggies your child needs in a day.

Resources

Please visit Anni's Conscious Family Living Web site at www.consciousfamilyliving.com. From there, you can link to her Web site for her first book: www.organicallyraisedcookbook.com, as well as a list of Anni's favorite bloggers and online stores. Anni's Web site offers recipes, tips on green and sustainable living, natural crafting projects, and a whole lot more.

Pop Molds

Chez Bettay: www.chezbettay.com sells Tovolo brand ice pop molds
Greenfeet: www.greenfeet.com sells BPA-Free ice pop molds
The Tickle Trunk: www.thetickletrunk.com sells stainless steel pop molds by Onyx (Anni's favorite ice pop molds)

Farms and Farmers' Markets

www.localharvest.org
www.pickyourown.org

Agave Nectar

Loving Earth/Agave Nectar: www.raw-chocolate.net
Madhava: www.madhavahoney.com sells raw agave nectar

Chocolate

Loving Earth: www.raw-chocolate.net
Nuts Online: www.nutsonline.com sells chocolate nibs
Raw Guru: www.rawguru.com sells raw chocolate

Coconut

Essential Living Foods: www.essentiallivingfoods.com sells coconut sugar
Living Tree Community: www.livingtreecommunity.com

Lavender Extract

Silver Cloud Estates: www.silvercloudestates.com

Tea

Chado Tea Room in Los Angeles: www.chadotea.com
Mountain Rose Herbs: www.mountainroseherbs.com
Radiance Tea House & Books in New York: http://radiancetea.com
Tea Spot in New York: www.teaspotnyc.com
Yogi Organic Teas: www.yogiproducts.com

References

(1) *BPA Info:*

http://www.ehow.com/how_2124117_buy-bpafree-sippy-cups.html

(2) *Wheat Germ:*

http://www.wisegeek.com/what-is-wheat-germ.htm

(3) *Cantaloupes:*

http://www.sundiafruit.com/SundiaFruits/Sundia-Cantaloupe/Funfacts.php

(4) *Yogurt:*

http://www.whfoods.com/genpage.php?tname=foodspice&dbid=124

(5) *Greek Yogurt:*

http://healthmad.com/nutrition/what-are-the-health-benefits-of-greek-yogurt-vs-regular-yogurt/

(6) *Tofu:*

http://www.veg-world.com/articles/tofu.htm

(7) *Coconut Water:*

http://www.associatedcontent.com/article/735177/seven_benefits_of_coconut_water.html?cat=5

(8) *Rooibos Tea:*

http://www.teabenefits.com/rooibos-tea-benefits.html

(9) *Chocolate:*

http://www.facts-about-chocolate.com/where-does-chocolate-come-from.html

(10) *Raw Chocolate:*

http://www.articlesbase.com/chocolate-articles/what-is-raw-chocolate-and-why-eat-it-985217.html

(11) *Dark Chocolate:*

http://www.webmd.com/diet/news/20030827/dark-chocolate-is-healthy-chocolate

(12) *Quinoa:*

http://www.whfoods.com/genpage.php?dbid=142&tname=foodspice

Index

Acknowledgments

Mom...I love you. Plain and simple, you are the very best.

Tim, my love, you have supported me, carried an ice chest full of ice pops all around town, edited my proposals, managed all of our children, and all with a smile on your face. Thank you and I love you more than you can possibly know.

Zoë, Lotus, Bodhi and River...I love you all so much. I am so proud of each of you and am honored to be your mommy!

To my new crew — Melanie, Ashley and Betsy — I love you gals and our Wednesday mornings. You keep me laughing and I honestly do not know what I would do without you mamas.

Thank you to all of my amazing ice pop models — Lotus, Bodhi, Zoë, Duke, Noah, Luke, Avery, Dahaven, Maya, Devyn, Cali, Fiona, Collin, Zoey, Grace, Olivia, Madeline, Ryan, Maddie, Pierce, Ryland, and Madison, and Sophia, Bella, and Joe (my pop assistants) — you rock!

Thank you, Highland Hall Waldorf School for the use of your gorgeous school for photographs and Dana for the use of your home and pool. Thanks, also, to Entertaining Elephants (entertainingelephants.com) for the use of your adorable clothing for some of our photoshoots.

Alexandra, my dear friend and goddess of photography, thank you for always showing up, rain or shine, and for the magic we create together. You are so amazing and talented and I love it when the shots are so gorgeous it literally hurts! I love you.

My editor, Megan, thank you for loving this project and for your ice pop vision and for realizing that pops are the new cupcakes!

My agent, Meredith, you are always in my corner...thanks so much for all of your hard work on all of my projects and for keeping up with me! I know that is hard sometimes...